DATE DUE

JUN 0 7 2010

DEMCO, INC. 38-2931

RULERS, SCHOLARS, AND ARTISTS OF THE RENAISSANCE™

ELIZABETH I

Queen of England's Golden Age

RULERS,
SCHOLARS, AND
ARTISTS OF THE
RENAISSANCE™

ELIZABETH I

Queen of England's Golden Age

Paul Hilliam

The Rosen Publishing Group, Inc., New York

To my wife

Published in 2005 by The Rosen Publishing Group, Inc.
29 East 21st Street, New York, NY 10010

Library of Congress Cataloging-in-Publication Data

Hilliam, Paul.
Elizabeth I: Queen of England's golden age/Paul Hilliam—1st ed.
    p. cm.—(Rulers, scholars, and artists of the Renaissance)
Includes bibliographical references and index.
ISBN 1-4042-0313-3 (library binding)
1. Elizabeth I, Queen of England, 1533–1603. 2. Great Britain—
History—Elizabeth, 1558–1603. 3. Queens—Great Britain—
Biography.
I. Title. II. Series.
DA355.H55 2005
942.05'5'092—dc22

                                                    2004010572

Manufactured in the United States of America

On the cover: Background: Whitehall, the former royal palace, painted by Antonio Canal from 1746 to 1747. Inset: A circa 1546 portrait of a teenage Elizabeth by William Scrots.

CONTENTS

INTRODUCTION

Elizabeth I lived from 1533 to 1603 and was queen of England for forty-five years. However, when she was a child, it seemed unlikely that she would ascend to the throne. During her long life, she encountered many personal difficulties but also enjoyed the love and respect of the people she ruled. Elizabethan England faced various problems as well, which the queen and her ministers did their best to tackle. Despite the fact that this period in English history was very turbulent and often violent, it was also full of memorable events and achievements and has become known as a golden age.

ELIZABETH'S EARLY LIFE

CHAPTER 1

Elizabeth was born on September 7, 1533, in the Palace of Greenwich on the banks of the river Thames, just east of London. Her mother, Anne Boleyn, was already pregnant with Elizabeth when she married King Henry VIII of England. The king looked forward to having a son, who in time would inherit his throne. However, Henry was bitterly disappointed that the birth resulted in a girl and soon lost interest in his new daughter.

THE PRINCESS ELIZABETH

Henry's marriage to Anne Boleyn was his second marriage, and it lasted only three years. Anne had won Henry's heart with her flirting, but when she failed to produce a son, the king soon grew tired of her proud,

This is the earliest surviving solo portrait of Elizabeth I, dating from circa 1546, when Elizabeth was a teenager. She is shown holding a book and marking her place, as if she has been interrupted in her reading. Another book appears open on a lectern on the left. These books are a symbol of the learning and intelligence for which Elizabeth was famed. Her rich and fashionable clothing clearly indicates her high status as the daughter of King Henry VIII. Elizabeth sent this portrait, painted by William Scrots, to her brother, King Edward VI, as a gift. It is now on public view at Windsor Castle.

bossy, and quarrelsome character. The king's closest adviser, Thomas Cromwell, disliked the new queen and persuaded Henry that Anne was unfaithful and had been involved in a series of affairs with other men. A fake trial declared Anne guilty, and she was beheaded. At the age of only two and a half, Elizabeth was left motherless, while her father disowned her. She was declared a bastard (a child born outside of marriage). To prevent her from becoming queen in the future, she was excluded from the line of succession to the throne. Her childhood was very lonely. She rarely saw her father and spent most of her time in the country at Hatfield House, north of London, where she was brought up by a governess.

Henry VIII's third wife, Jane Seymour, gave birth to Prince Edward in 1537, and Jane died soon afterward. Prince Edward and Princess Elizabeth got on well and were given the same tutor. Elizabeth studied Italian, French, Latin, and Greek. Reports of her progress showed that she was a keen, bright pupil. She also developed into a good-looking girl with light red hair and a lively sense of fun.

Elizabeth's life became happier for a while, especially when her brother became King Edward VI in 1547, at the age of nine. However, Edward was a sickly child and he died at age fifteen in 1553. The

King Edward VI died at Greenwich Palace (seen above in a 1767 drawing) on July 6, 1553. When Elizabeth, who was born in Greenwich Palace in 1533, became queen, she made the palace her principal residence.

crown next passed to Elizabeth's half-sister, Mary, daughter of Henry VIII and his first wife, Catherine of Aragon.

THE EARLIER TUDOR MONARCHS

Elizabeth's early life was full of danger and uncertainty until she became queen in 1558. This was particularly true during the reign of her half-sister, Mary. Elizabeth's path to the throne and some of the key events in her long reign are rooted in the lives of the earlier Tudor monarchs, so it is worth a brief look at their reigns and how they directly affected Elizabeth. The term "Tudor" refers to the royal house (or family) that ruled England from 1485 to 1603.

HENRY VII (REIGNED 1485–1509)

In 1485, Elizabeth's grandfather Henry Tudor VII (a Welshman) defeated King Richard III at the Battle of Bosworth. This was the final battle in the so-called Wars of the Roses, which had been fought over a long period of time between two rival houses (or groups of nobles) known as York and Lancaster. Lancaster won, and Henry founded the Tudor dynasty, which lasted until Elizabeth's death in 1603. Henry VII united the red and white roses (symbols of the two houses) and helped end the feud by marrying Elizabeth, daughter of the Yorkist monarch, Edward IV.

HENRY VIII (REIGNED 1509–1547)

Two weeks before his coronation, Henry VIII kept a promise he had made to his father and married Catherine of Aragon, his elder brother's Spanish widow. In 1516, Catherine gave birth to a daughter named Mary, but Henry became increasingly desperate for a son. After Catherine suffered a series of miscarriages, Henry divorced her, and she spent the rest of her days in a nunnery.

Henry then married Anne Boleyn, who was already pregnant with Elizabeth. When Anne was beheaded for alleged unfaithfulness, Henry next married Jane Seymour, who died shortly after giving birth to Prince Edward. Henry married three more times, but fathered no more children.

Although Henry's love life and family dramas are fascinating, the most significant feature of his reign was the start of the Protestant Reformation. Until this point, England had been a Catholic country in which ordinary people, priests, monks, and even the king and queen regarded the pope as their religious leader. Because Pope Clement VII refused to grant a divorce to Henry and Catherine, the king decided to do away with the pope's influence. In 1534, he made himself supreme head of the new Church of England. In most respects, the Church of England did not differ greatly from the Catholic Church, but it was independent of the pope. The king was its ultimate authority. This sent England on the road to adopting a Protestant style of Christianity. In addition, the Catholic monasteries were all closed, and their wealth and lands were seized by the king.

Henry VIII sits enthroned surrounded by his family. At far left is his daughter, Mary, by his first wife, Catherine of Aragon. The young boy by Henry's side is his son, Edward, by his third wife, Jane Seymour, who stands to Henry's left. At far right is Elizabeth, Henry's daughter by his second wife, Anne Boleyn. This is the earliest known depiction of Elizabeth, the future queen of England.

EDWARD VI (REIGNED 1547–1553)

Elizabeth was fourteen when Henry VIII died and her younger brother, Prince Edward, became King Edward VI at the age of nine. Elizabeth was pleased to return from her exile at Hatfield House to live in the royal court in London. However, Edward's reign brought its own particular difficulties for Elizabeth.

Because Edward was too young to rule, the country was really governed by a council led by the Duke of Somerset (Edward's uncle). The duke's younger brother, Lord Thomas Seymour, married Katherine Parr (Henry VIII's sixth wife) and through this marriage started to become close to the young Princess Elizabeth, who was friends with Katherine. After Katherine's death in 1548, Thomas became hungry for power and plotted to marry the fifteen-year-old Princess Elizabeth. She may have been a little in love with Thomas. Eventually, though, she saw through his scheming and denied that they had been involved in any relationship. Meanwhile, the Duke of Somerset also made himself unpopular by ordering the execution of his brother Thomas.

Edward VI was not a healthy boy and died in 1553, at the age of fifteen. He may have suffered from tuberculosis, an often fatal lung disease. The most significant features of his short reign were that

Protestantism became more firmly established across England, and money from the closure of the Catholic monasteries was used to found several grammar schools.

LADY JANE GREY (REIGNED FOR NINE DAYS IN 1553)

One of England's most powerful nobles, the Duke of Northumberland, plotted to have Edward VI succeeded by Lady Jane Grey, who was Elizabeth's second cousin. Northumberland was motivated partly by the fear that England would become Catholic again if Mary, Henry VIII's eldest daughter, became queen. Edward VI's will stated that neither of his sisters, Mary or Elizabeth, were to become the next monarch because they were women. Northumberland saw in this situation an opportunity for personal gain and influence. In 1553, Jane, aged fifteen and a great-granddaughter of Henry VII, was forced to marry Northumberland's son, Guildford Dudley. Some thought that Jane, a Protestant, might be a more acceptable successor to Edward. However, Jane was not actually crowned and her reign lasted only nine days. Northumberland, Jane, and Guildford were all executed by Mary once she seized the throne.

MARY I (REIGNED 1553–1558)

Mary had been declared an illegitimate child when her mother, Catherine of Aragon, was banished from Henry VIII's court. As a Catholic and a woman, she did not expect to succeed to the throne. When she did become queen, however, her main ambition was to restore Catholicism in England, first by producing a Catholic male heir and second by reversing the Protestant Reformation started by her father and continued by her half-brother Edward VI.

Mary was thirty-seven when she became queen. English Protestants were horrified when she decided to marry her Catholic cousin, Prince Philip of Spain. The marriage seemed to indicate that Catholicism would again be imposed by force on the country. Eighteen months after the marriage in Winchester Cathedral, Philip returned to Spain. It was a political marriage, arranged to strengthen relations between England and Spain, but Philip obviously disliked Mary. Although it was not a union of love, Mary thought that she was pregnant. The symptoms from which she was suffering, however, were actually those of a dreadful disease, and Mary remained childless. Meanwhile "Bloody Mary" gave prominent Protestants the choice of "turn or burn." She forced hundreds of Protestants to either reconvert to

Mary Tudor married Prince Philip II in 1554. As a Catholic queen of England—an increasingly Protestant country—she felt great pressure to marry and have children in order to ensure that her descendants would continue to rule England as a Catholic nation. Mary was thirty-seven years old when she married and was never able to conceive a child. Eighteen months after his wedding, Philip deserted her and returned to Spain.

Catholicism or be burned at the stake. In total, she ordered that 288 people be burned to death because they refused to reconvert to Catholicism.

During Mary's reign, Elizabeth became the focus of Protestant hopes of rebellion. In 1554, a soldier named Sir Thomas Wyatt, tried to raise a revolt against Mary when she pro-posed marriage to Philip of Spain. Letters from Wyatt to Elizabeth were discovered and taken as proof of a plot against Mary. Elizabeth was sent to prison in the Tower of London and accused of treason.

At first, Elizabeth refused to enter the tower by Traitors' Gate, the gate through which enemies of the crown were forced to pass. She sat weeping on a

On March 16, 1554, Elizabeth wrote this letter to her half-sister, Mary Tudor, defending herself against charges of participating in Sir Thomas Wyatt's rebellion against the Catholic queen. Written just after she learned that she was to be imprisoned in the Tower of London—"a place more wanted for a false traitor than a true subject"—Elizabeth insists that "I never practised, counselled, nor consented to anything that might be prejudicial to your person anyway, or dangerous to the state by any means." The letter apparently failed to move Mary, who kept Elizabeth in the tower for three months.

stone beside the river Thames, sobbing, "I am come in no traitor, but as a true woman to the queen's majesty" (as quoted in Neville Williams's *The Life and Times of Elizabeth I*). She humbly pleaded her innocence. After three months, she was released, though Mary continued to be dismayed that Elizabeth would not convert to Catholicism. When Mary died in 1558, neither Elizabeth nor the majority of people in England were sorry.

ELIZABETH BECOMES QUEEN

With the death of Queen Mary, the throne passed peacefully to Elizabeth. People were pleased that the religious persecutions during Mary's reign were at an end. On the afternoon that she died, bells rang throughout London and people even set up tables and feasted in the streets. Elizabeth was sitting under an oak tree, reading a prayer book when she heard the news and is reported to have said, "It is the Lord's doing and it is marvelous in our eyes" (as quoted in Alison Weir's *Elizabeth the Queen*). Soon she set out from Hatfield House to London, where she was enthusiastically greeted by large crowds.

Nevertheless, Elizabeth knew that she had inherited a country in which there were deep divisions and real problems. One of the biggest problems

A small portrait of Elizabeth I appears within the illuminated capital letter *p* in this 1572 law document. Illuminated manuscripts of the medieval and early Renaissance era feature elaborate designs, miniature pictures, and vibrant colors, including gold and silver. Elizabeth is depicted holding an orb with a cross rising from its top. This represents the Christian rule of the queen. She also holds the great sword of state, symbolizing the sovereign's royal authority.

that Elizabeth faced was that she was not a man. This may seem strange in these days of equal opportunity for men and women, but many of Elizabeth's subjects would have preferred a king. People believed that the problems associated with Mary's reign stemmed partly from the fact that she was Catholic, but also from the fact that she was a woman. Elizabeth was aware that she had to create and project an image of strength and steadfastness that would overcome this difficulty.

ELIZABETH'S CORONATION

There was a little snow in the air as Elizabeth's magnificent procession made its way to Westminster Abbey for the coronation on January 15, 1559. She wore a gold robe, smiled and waved at the crowds, and asked that her coach might stop from time to time so that she could accept presents from her new subjects as she passed by. The new queen certainly knew how to capture the hearts of her people.

There was difficulty in finding a suitable senior bishop to perform the actual coronation ceremony, because Mary's persecution of Protestants had left many cathedral posts vacant. The duty was eventually given to the relatively unimportant bishop of

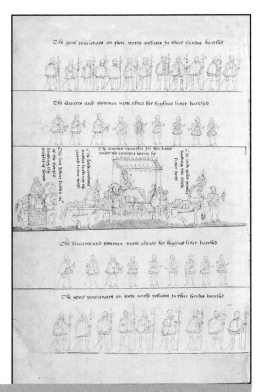

Carlisle. After the coronation service, a feast was held, during which a knight, known as the queen's champion, rode into Westminster Hall in full armor to challenge any enemies of the new monarch to come forward and fight. None presented themselves for the offered contest.

Queen Elizabeth's coronation festivities began on January 14, 1559, when she was carried through the crowded London streets on a golden litter (a covered and curtained couch carried by servants). This sixteenth-century drawing commemorates Elizabeth's coronation procession. The top and bottom pair of panels depict the men-at-arms (royal guards), squires, and footmen who attended the queen during the procession. The queen herself is seen in her litter in the middle panel. Lord Robert Dudley, the queen's longtime friend and favorite, appears on the horse to her left.

GOVERNMENT, HOUSEHOLD, AND COURT

Following the coronation festivities, Elizabeth set about planning how best to govern the country. Although only twenty-five, she was a highly intelligent young woman who showed herself to be shrewd and diplomatic as she chose her ministers. Mary had been guided by the Privy Council (a group of officials who advised the king or queen). However, the new queen felt that the council had been too large and politically divided, so she dismissed two-thirds of its members and replaced them with her own relations, servants, and political allies, led by William Cecil. Only the most able ministers of Mary's government were kept.

In her household and court, Elizabeth surrounded herself with those she knew she could trust, including her late mother's relatives and her own domestic staff. The queen was therefore able to rely on people, most of them Protestants, who were personally loyal to her. William Cecil was first appointed chief secretary of state in 1559, and then Lord High Treasurer in 1572. He remained as Elizabeth's chief minister for forty years and was rewarded with the title of Lord Burghley when he retired.

A "MERE WOMAN"

Some men related the problems of Mary's reign to the supposed "weakness" of her sex. She was a "mere woman." At this time, women were thought to have been created by God to fulfill particular roles and be subservient to men because they were

Elizabeth I is depicted at prayer in this 1569 illustration. The image appeared opposite the title page of her personal prayer book. In 1559, soon after Elizabeth became queen, the Church of England's prayer book was revised in order to ease tensions with England's Catholic minority. The prayer book was made less Protestant in spirit by, for example, the removal of prayers against the pope and by the addition of some saints' days and festivals. The Elizabethan prayer book was the first one used in North America, brought there by the Jamestown settlers and others in the early 1600s.

seen as physically, emotionally, and intellectually inferior. Yet, it would seem God had allowed Englishmen to be governed again by a woman.

Elizabeth did all she could to overcome being regarded as a "mere woman." She constantly stressed that she was the daughter of Henry VIII, whom people remembered as a firm, decisive ruler. In 1559, she told Parliament that she hoped "to keep this our realm in as good justice, peace and rest, in like wise as the king my father held in you" (according to the rolls—or records—of Parliament).

Sometimes, however, Elizabeth gave the impression of being a "mere woman" when it suited her purposes—to inspire the loyalty, support, and service of her subjects. In 1563, she described herself to Parliament as "being a woman, wanting both wit and memory." This was, of course, just tactical false modesty, as Elizabeth was highly intelligent and possessed a strong understanding of government affairs. When she received foreign ambassadors, she often spoke to them in their own languages, since she was fluent in Latin, French, and Italian. Her studies as a child were certainly put to good use in Elizabeth's role as queen of England.

Some supporters of the queen argued that Elizabeth had been given special qualities by God in order to fulfill his divine purpose. She ruled by divine right and the peace and prosperity during her reign proved that she was on the throne because God willed it. Elizabeth's favor with God, it was argued, made up for the fact that she was not a male monarch. Even Elizabeth came to regard herself as a "special woman" rather than a "mere woman," and Cecil, her chief minister, came to see her as exceptional, too.

Nearly everyone believed that the best way to "compensate" for Elizabeth's gender would be through marriage and the production of a male heir to the throne. Meanwhile, the queen made every effort to portray herself in a positive way.

GLORIANA

One way Elizabeth presented herself to her subjects was by making "royal progresses" through her kingdom. These were tours, usually in the south or center of the country, which lasted for weeks or even months, during which she stayed at the homes of her nobles and courtiers, at their expense. Records list 241 places where she stayed during these tours. Four hundred carts and 2,400 packhorses were required to carry the royal luggage! Entertaining the queen, the large number of servants and courtiers with whom she traveled cost huge amounts of money, and

From September 20 through September 23, 1591, Edward Seymour, the Earl of Hertford, entertained Queen Elizabeth I at Elvetham in Hampshire, England, along with her retinue of about 400. In order to entertain her with an impressive spectacle, the earl dug a crescent-shaped lake in his park. The manmade lake featured islands and boats and served as the backdrop for a four-day pageant depicting a battle between the four elements—earth, air, water, and fire. This 1591 wood engraving records the Elvetham spectacle enjoyed by Elizabeth.

several of her hosts suffered bankruptcy as a result of her visits.

In 1575, Elizabeth's favorite nobleman, Robert Dudley, who was the Earl of Leicester, staged a huge entertainment at Kenilworth Castle, with plays, dances, pageants, and fireworks lasting for nineteen days. When the Earl of Hertford learned that Elizabeth was coming to stay on his estate, he employed 300 men to build extra rooms and dig a lake in his garden for the queen's pleasure! During these progresses, Elizabeth would make impromptu speeches to crowds of ordinary folk and make a great show of graciously accepting even the most humble presents given to her.

Playwrights and poets also flattered the queen and inflated her image by describing her in mythological terms. In his epic poem *The Faerie Queen*, Edmund Spenser created a character named Gloriana who represents Elizabeth. Gloriana is a bright and graceful goddess, a "Great Lady of the greatest Isle." A popular nickname for the queen was Astraea. The Roman poet Ovid was the first to write about a goddess named Astraea who, it was thought, would return to Earth to proclaim a golden age, after having left in disgust because of war and evil. In time, people did indeed look back on Elizabeth's reign as a golden age.

THE VIRGIN QUEEN

When Elizabeth was crowned queen, everyone in England expected that she would soon marry. Producing a prince who would later become the next king was regarded by many as a priority. So in 1559, Parliament spoke to the queen about her need to marry and produce an heir. Her ministers then went on to discuss the limitations to be placed on the powers of her future husband. At this stage, nobody imagined that Elizabeth would remain single. After all, as a princess, various eligible men had expressed an interest in marrying her, including Archduke Ferdinand of Austria, the Duke of Savoy (from Italy), and the Crown Prince of Sweden.

ELIZABETH'S EARLY SUITORS

At the start of Elizabeth's reign, King Philip II of Spain sent one of his nobles to the queen to offer Philip's hand in marriage. Philip had, of course, been married to Elizabeth's half-sister, Queen Mary. He made it clear that he wished to relieve his sister-in-law of the burden of rule. However, it was obvious that his proposal was politically motivated. At this time, Spain was particularly interested in gaining influence over England, partly to protect shipping routes along the English Channel to Spanish dominions in the Netherlands. In addition, Philip II was a devout Catholic and saw it as his solemn duty to spread Catholicism as widely as possible.

In 1563, Parliament again spoke to the queen, asking her to let "God incline your Majesty's heart to marriage, and that he will so bless and send such good success thereunto that we may see the fruit and child that may come thereof," according to Parliament records. Further pleas came in 1566 and 1576. It was argued that a royal husband was an unfortunate necessity: the real aim was to produce a royal son. The queen accepted that she had a duty to marry for the good of the realm. She told Parliament that although she would prefer to stay single, she would marry for the sake of her subjects. The truth was that she was enjoying ruling and being her own master! A husband would not only want to rule the country, but also to control her.

Despite wanting to settle the question of who would succeed her as the next monarch, Elizabeth's ministers felt that there was nothing to gain from a future male monarch. If Elizabeth did marry, they were intent on limiting her husband's powers because they stood to lose influence

This illuminated manuscript shows Philip II and Mary Tudor enthroned as king and queen of England. Thanks to his marriage to Mary, the Spanish king Philip was able to form an alliance with England, an arrangement he hoped to continue by also marrying Elizabeth, his late wife's half-sister.

for themselves once he became king and installed his own advisers.

Meanwhile, there were plenty of suitors. The Earl of Arundel borrowed vast sums of money to

stage impressive entertainments for the queen when she visited him, and even tried to bribe the queen's servants and friends to persuade her to marry him. King Erik of Sweden sent his brother to plead on his behalf. The Earl of Arran (in Scotland), the Dukes of Holstein and Saxony (in Germany), and the Archduke of Austria all made inquiries. The growing number of hopeful candidates became an embarrassment, and circulating printed pictures of the queen with various suitors was banned.

ROBERT DUDLEY, EARL OF LEICESTER

Elizabeth was not entirely beyond the reach of romance, however. The courtship that came nearest to creating a scandal was between the queen and Robert Dudley, whom she made the Earl of Leicester. Although the exact nature of their relationship is

This engraving, *Queen Elizabeth in Parliament*, appears next to the title page of a book published in London in 1682, entitled *The Journals of all the Parliaments during the Reign of Queen Elizabeth, Both of the House of Lords and House of Commons*. Elizabeth generally enjoyed good relations with Parliament, many of whose members had great affection for the queen. Throughout Elizabeth's reign, however, Parliament continuously pressed her on issues of religion, her marriage plans, and her successor.

uncertain, he was probably the only man Elizabeth ever really loved. It was obvious that Elizabeth very much enjoyed his company, but whether she seriously considered marrying him is difficult to determine. Nevertheless, during the summer of 1560, they spent days on end alone together, during which time the queen ignored her ministers and various responsibilities.

The main stumbling block to the relationship was the fact that Robert Dudley was already married. However, in the summer of 1560, Robert's wife, Amy, was reported to be dying of breast cancer. Soon there was talk that the queen and Robert were planning to marry.

Cecil, Elizabeth's chief minister, disapproved of the relationship, not only because Dudley was married, but also because he was widely distrusted. His father, the Duke of Northumberland, had been executed during the reign of Queen Mary for plotting to marry his eldest son to Lady Jane Grey (Elizabeth's cousin) and put her on the throne. Cecil made plans to resign as secretary of state if Elizabeth and Dudley married. Hoping to head off this possibility, however, he also plotted to prevent the marriage by spreading a rumor that Amy Dudley was not really ill at all, but that Elizabeth and Robert were plotting to poison her. Cecil told this story to the Spanish ambassador, adding that Dudley was bringing disaster to the realm.

Cecil's devious tactics had two results. First, the ambassador warned the queen against the marriage. Second, when Amy did die in September 1560, Robert was suspected of arranging her murder. She had been found home alone, lying dead at the bottom of some stairs with a broken neck. Elizabeth sent Dudley away from court while an inquiry was made into the circumstances surrounding his wife's death. Although he was eventually found to be innocent, marriage between Dudley and the queen now seemed impossible.

William Cecil served Elizabeth I for forty years as secretary of state and lord treasurer. He went on to become Elizabeth's chief spokesperson and administrative head of her government. His most important role was serving as liaison between the Queen and Parliament, especially on religious matters.

The taint of scandal clung to Dudley despite his apparent innocence.

Elizabeth continued to be fond of Dudley and, in 1564, conferred upon him the title Earl of Leicester. When he died in 1588, the queen was visibly upset.

CHOOSING TO STAY SINGLE

As the years passed and her relationship with Dudley generated increasing opposition, Elizabeth began to recognize the likelihood that she would not marry. Nevertheless, courtship for the royal hand in marriage continued, during which time Elizabeth seemed prepared to offer herself to the highest bidder. However, the queen's political demands were always too high, and in every case she looked for the pitfalls in a possible marriage, rather than the advantages. Only the Duke of Alençon (from France) seems to have been considered with any seriousness, but he was rejected because he was thought to be too Catholic.

The queen told a royal envoy, "If I follow the inclination of my nature, it is this: beggar-woman and single, far rather than queen and married!" (as quoted in the rolls of Parliament). She told the Spanish ambassador that she would stay single if she could find an acceptable way of settling the question of succession. On one hand Elizabeth felt she could not marry one of her subjects because it would be beneath her. On the other hand, she would not marry a foreign prince or noble because she stood to lose her own power. She remembered all too well how marital problems had disrupted the reigns of her father, Henry VIII and her half-sister, Mary.

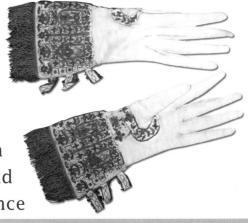

These gloves were presented to Queen Elizabeth I on a visit to Oxford in 1566. It was customary to present royal visitors with several pairs of gloves but, for some reason, the queen left this pair behind. They are now housed at the Ashmolean Museum of Art and Archaeology at the University of Oxford.

Elizabeth turned her unmarried state to her advantage. In a sense, she was regarded as being married to all of her subjects and even to the kingdom of England. The queen's supposed virginity led people to compare her to the Virgin Mary, and it was even said that when Elizabeth died, she would be the second maid in heaven.

RELIGION IN ELIZABETHAN ENGLAND

CHAPTER 4

When Elizabeth became queen in 1558, she inherited a country in which there was deep religious division. Under Elizabeth's father, Henry VIII, the country had split from the Catholic Church and established the independent Church of England (also known as the Anglican Church). This development was part of the larger Protestant movement sweeping across Europe, led by a former Catholic priest in Germany named Martin Luther. Then, during Mary's bloody reign, England became Catholic once again. Upon reaching the throne herself, Elizabeth made it her aim to stop religious persecution and create a settlement, or "middle way," which she hoped would satisfy the majority of her subjects, both Catholics and Protestants.

A NATION DIVIDED

Mary I had been a zealous Catholic. The religious persecutions during her reign had resulted in attempted forced conversions that involved torture. Hundreds who refused to convert were burned at the stake. Many Protestants became "Marian exiles" because they fled during Mary's reign to Protestant countries such as Germany (where Martin Luther had begun the growing Protestant Reformation) and Switzerland (where John Calvin had also led a Protestant movement).

Elizabeth had received a Protestant upbringing and education. She disagreed with Catholic doctrines, or beliefs. In particular, she did not believe in transubstantiation—the belief that the wine and bread at the Catholic Mass change into the actual blood and body of Jesus Christ. She did, however, enjoy some of the ceremonial and traditional aspects of Catholicism, such as the administration of bishops and the placing of crucifixes above altars. Nevertheless, it was obvious that Elizabeth intended to go even further than her father had in establishing a Protestant Church in England that differed considerably from the Catholic Church.

After King Philip of Spain wed fellow Catholic and queen of England Mary Tudor, they tried to force England to return to Catholicism. Beginning in February 1555, they tracked down those who had been active Protestants during the previous reign of Edward VI and ordered them to be publicly burned to death. These burnings *(pictured above)* went on and on in many cities across England throughout the rest of Mary's reign.

It is difficult to know how many Protestants and Catholics there were in England when Elizabeth came to the throne in 1558. It is probable that the farther north from London one went, the more Catholics there were. However, Elizabeth's new Privy Council, led by William Cecil, was strongly Protestant. A number of its members had been educated at Cambridge and were members of a Protestant society called the Athenians.

There was great fear in England that the pope would effectively rule the country if England remained Catholic. At the same time, there was also fear of a Catholic invasion from abroad if England again embraced Protestantism. At the time, Scotland was ruled by a Catholic, Mary Queen of Scots. She had strong links with France because she had married the French dauphin (heir to the French throne), who was also Catholic. The French king Henry II declared Mary the rightful ruler of England, because she was the great-granddaughter of Henry VII of England. As a consequence of this Catholic alliance between Scotland and France, Elizabeth and her ministers worried that these two countries might unite and invade England from the north and south. It was also the case at this time that the French port of Calais, previously owned by England, had been lost to the French during the reign of Mary I. This strategic port offered the French a useful launching point for any attempted invasion of England.

Support for England came from an unexpected source. The Spanish king Philip II (Catholic and pre-viously married to Mary I of England) was at war with France. He feared that a conquest of England

John Calvin was raised in a strict Roman Catholic family. His father wanted John to become a priest, but John instead fell under the influence of Protestantism. In 1533, after completing a law degree from the University of Paris, Calvin fled the city after it became known that he was associating with individuals who opposed the Catholic Church. Calvin eventually traveled to Protestant-friendly Geneva, Switzerland. He spent most of his remaining years there until his death in 1564, lecturing on and preaching the Protestant faith. Calvinism became the majority denomination in Scotland, the Netherlands, and parts of Germany, and was influential in France, Hungary, and Poland. Most settlers in the American mid-Atlantic and New England were Calvinists as well, including the Puritans and Dutch settlers of New Amsterdam (New York).

by Scotland and France would prevent trade between Spain and the Spanish Netherlands. He therefore saw a benefit in keeping England as an ally and offered to marry Elizabeth. She kept him waiting by neither accepting his offer nor flatly refusing. More important, though, the Spanish king tried to maintain the balance of political power in Europe by threatening to invade France if Henry II invaded England.

Meanwhile, Scotland was undergoing its own Protestant movement, led by John Knox. After the Protestants gained power in Scotland, the 1560 Treaty of Edinburgh, signed by England and Scotland, brought peace between the two countries for the next 100 years and broke the "auld alliance" between Scotland and France.

THE ELIZABETHAN SETTLEMENT

As the threat of a Catholic invasion temporarily lifted, Elizabeth seized the opportunity that peace and stability offered and attempted to settle religious affairs in England. Her aim was first to stop the threat of papal interference by appointing herself supreme governor of the Church of England, and second to create a Protestant England in which there was a measure of toleration for other religious denominations. The Elizabethan church had become a largely successful compromise containing elements of the Calvinist, Lutheran, and Catholic churches. In its beliefs, it was Protestant, but in its administrative and outward structure, it was still heavily influenced by Catholicism, with priests, bishops, and cathedrals ministering to the faithful. In this new climate of tolerance, Protestant exiles started to return to England.

Early in February 1559, Elizabeth's council introduced a series of bills into the House of Commons. The Act of Supremacy made Elizabeth supreme governor of the Church of England. Elizabeth aimed to bring back the style of church services that had been used until the time of her younger brother, Edward VI. The Act of Uniformity, also passed in 1559, imposed compulsory church attendance for everyone on Sundays and enforced the use of a new prayer book (based on one issued in 1552) as the prescribed type of worship for the whole country. The style of the new prayer book was Protestant, but it was carefully and sensitively written in the hope that the wording used for the service of Communion would be acceptable to Catholics. Many Catholics were still unhappy and felt persecuted by the enforced Protestant worship and the outlawing of Catholic Mass. They continued

celebrating Mass se-
cretly, using their old
liturgy, or service books.

THE ARRIVAL OF THE JESUITS AND THE CATHOLIC MISSION IN ENGLAND

In 1570, the pope ex-
communicated Queen
Elizabeth. According to
the pope, she could no
longer legitimately be
queen if she was not
Catholic. Excommun-
ication is the most

Ignatius Loyola was the founder of the Society of Jesus, also known as the Jesuit Order. Devoted to obedience and the missionary life, Jesuits made vows never to marry or own personal posses-sions. They also spread Catholic teaching anywhere it was unknown or unfamiliar.

serious punishment that the Catholic Church can
give. It means that a person cannot receive Holy
Communion—the consecrated bread and wine said
to be the body and blood of Jesus Christ. Anyone
who dies after being excommunicated is thought to
go straight to hell and be forever beyond the hope
of salvation.

As Protestantism became firmly established in England, Catholics in other European countries produced pictures, etchings, and woodcuts showing Catholics being tortured in England. As a result, in 1574, Catholics from Europe began to arrive in England on a mission to reconvert the country. Then, in 1580, a new Catholic missionary order known as the Society of Jesus sent some of its members, known as Jesuits, to England to join other Catholics in the reconversion mission. The Jesuits encouraged Catholics not to attend Protestant services. Those who avoided Protestant services became known as recusants, and their growing number alarmed Parliament. If the pope was calling upon Catholics to resist or even rise up against the queen, people began to ask whether the Catholics in their midst could be trusted.

In 1581, Parliament introduced heavy fines for Catholics not attending Church of England services, and people were imprisoned for not paying the fines. Rich Catholic families did their best to hide Catholic priests. The hiding places they created in their homes became known as priest holes. Finally, in 1585, came an act forbidding Jesuits to enter the country. Many Jesuits who remained in England were executed.

PURITANS

England became Protestant at the start of Elizabeth's reign with the Religious Settlement. Although this created a "middle of the road" church, there remained people, called Puritans, who wanted more radical reform of the Church of England. Some of these people were Marian exiles who returned to England after the death of Queen Mary. Prominent Puritans in the government included the Earl of Leicester (the queen's favorite) and his brother, the Earl of Warwick.

Some hard-line Puritans wanted immediate change, while others were prepared to wait patiently and introduce reforms gradually. All Puritans, however, wanted a total break from the Catholic past. In particular, they wanted simple services free from pomp and ceremony, the removal from churches of pictures and statues (which they viewed as encouraging idol worship), and greater emphasis placed on the Bible within services. They also thought that their faith should influence every part of their lives, and that a religion that only expected people to attend services each Sunday was not enough. The Puritans called each other "true gospellers" or the "godly."

A seventeenth-century English Puritan walks past a group of drinking men with less rigid standards of morality in this woodcut. Puritanism was a political and religious movement that sought to purify and reform the Church of England, mostly by doing away with church hierarchy and creating self-governing individual congregations. Puritans were intensely committed to a morality, a form of worship, and a society based strictly on the Ten Commandments. Puritanism reached North America with the English settlers who founded Plymouth Colony in 1620. It remained the dominant religious force in New England throughout the seventeenth and eighteenth centuries.

Puritanism reached a major stumbling block in 1588, with the death of the Earl of Leicester, the queen's favorite and a leading Puritan. In 1593, Parliament passed an act that threatened exile for anyone who refused to go to church on Sunday and was found to participate in a Puritan service. Puritanical exiles returning without permission were hanged. Before long, Puritans started to journey to America to escape this persecution and start a new life in a new world.

By 1589, Elizabeth was able to tell Parliament that she was "most fully and firmly settled in her conscience, by the work of God, that the estate and government of this Church of England, as it now standeth in this reformation, may justly be compared to any church which hath been established in any Christian Kingdom since the Apostles' time" (as quoted in the rolls of Parliament).

ELIZABETHAN CULTURE AND SOCIETY

During Elizabeth's long reign, England enjoyed a period of relative peace and stability, which allowed the arts to flourish. However, while some people, including the queen, enjoyed the artistic developments in theater, music, and painting, less fortunate members of society led lives characterized by poverty and misery.

THE THEATER

The second half of Elizabeth's reign is often referred to as the Golden Age of Theater. During Elizabeth's reign, professional companies of actors began to form. Part of the reason for this was that grammar schools had become an important feature of Tudor times, and they were producing a new

middle class of edu-
cated, creative, and
ambitious men. Many
of the growing theater
world's actors, man-
agers, and playwrights
came from this back-
ground and started to
make their mark in
Elizabethan England.

These new acting
companies were gran-
ted royal licenses,
giving them permission
to perform under the
patronage of specific
noblemen. The first of
these was Leicester's
Company, which was
licensed in 1574. Before
the construction of per-

This engraving of The Globe theater was made by the Amsterdam
artist Claes Jansz Visscher in
1616, the year of William
Shakespeare's death. The Globe
was designed and built by Richard
Burbage in 1599. Shakespeare
wrote and first presented many of
his greatest plays here.

manent theaters in London, acting companies
performed at royal palaces and toured throughout
the country. Plays were often performed on tempo-
rary wooden stages erected in inn courtyards, where
people could drink as they watched, either standing
or leaning out of windows. The most famous company

was called the Chamberlain's Men. It was run by a man named James Burbage, and a little-known actor named William Shakespeare became the group's chief playwright.

The first building devoted exclusively to plays was built by James Burbage and opened in 1576. It was called The Theatre because it was modeled after the shape of old Roman amphitheaters. Soon, rival theaters began appearing, such as The Swan and The Rose. Burbage himself built another venue, The Curtain. Later, his son Richard built The Globe. All of these new theaters were round and open to the sky. Admission cost one penny to stand in front of the stage (these audience members were called groundlings), or two pennies for those who wished to sit in a covered gallery. Playwrights such as Shakespeare, Christopher Marlowe, and Ben Jonson wrote the first English language plays and pro-duced some of the greatest drama—in any language—of all time.

SHAKESPEARE AND MARLOWE

William Shakespeare (1564–1616) and Christopher Marlowe (1564–1593) are considered the outstanding playwrights of the Elizabethan era. Shakespeare was born in Stratford-upon-Avon and came to London to seek his fortune in the 1580s. He first became an actor and may have joined Leicester's Company in 1587. In 1592, he started to write his own blank (unrhymed) verse plays. This was an unusual step for an actor to take in those days.

Shakespeare produced some of his most mature and accomplished plays, such as *Macbeth*, after 1603, during the reign of James I, Elizabeth's successor. However, during the last years of Elizabeth's reign, his plays included the

William Shakespeare is thought to be the subject of this painting, the so-called Hampton Court portrait. King William IV (1765–1837) bought the painting with the understanding that it was a Shakespeare portrait. If the man is indeed Shakespeare, he appears to be in stage dress, costumed as a soldier.

enduringly popular *Romeo and Juliet, A Midsummer Night's Dream, The Merchant of Venice, Hamlet*, and *Julius Caesar*. His plays fall broadly into three categories: comedy, tragedy, and history. He also wrote short poems called sonnets. His plays introduced entirely new vocabulary and

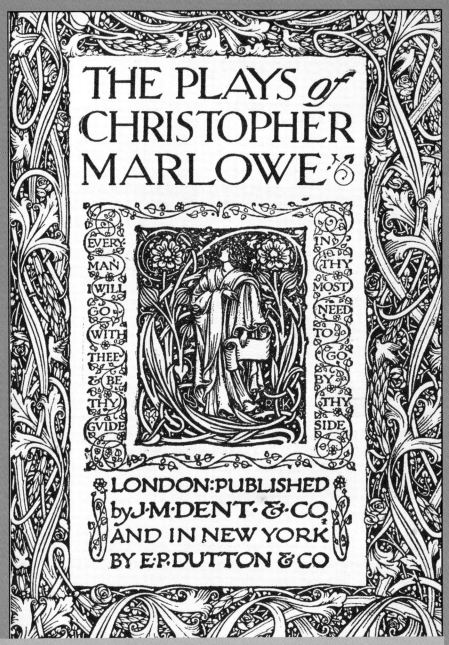

THE PLAYS *of* CHRISTOPHER MARLOWE

EVERY MAN I WILL GO WITH THEE & BE THY GVIDE

IN THY MOST NEED TO GO BY THY SIDE

LONDON: PUBLISHED by J·M·DENT·&·CO. AND IN NEW YORK BY E·P·DUTTON & CO

Christopher Marlowe is generally thought of as the greatest English dramatist before Shakespeare. They were born in the same year, but Marlowe died at the age of twenty-nine after a barroom stabbing. He had been notorious for his wild lifestyle and anti-religious views. He seemed to always court danger and was even engaged as a government spy for Queen Elizabeth. His 1588 play, *Dr. Faustus,* is considered his greatest work. Marlowe's death in 1593 came at the beginning of Shakespeare's own writing career, and therefore Shakespeare was suddenly left with no serious rivals. As a result, he became London's foremost playwright. Above is the title page from a collection of Marlowe's plays.

phrases into the English language, which we still use today. For example, to be "tongue-tied," to have "too much of a good thing," and to "vanish into thin air" are all phrases first used by Shakespeare.

Christopher Marlowe was born in Canterbury. He had the advantage of a university education, so although he would have been capable of writing his plays in Latin, as was the tradition, he chose to write blank verse in English. He felt that English plays were more accessible and therefore more exciting for his audience. Shakespeare admired Marlowe's plays, partly because they contained plenty of action. Marlowe's most well-known plays include *Tamburlaine* (the story of a cruel Asian conqueror), *Dr. Faustus* (about a man who sells his soul to the devil in return for forbidden knowledge and power on Earth), and *The Jew of Malta* (about a Jewish merchant's attempted revenge for the governor of Malta's seizure of his property). He led a fairly wild life and was killed during a fight in a tavern.

ENEMIES OF THE THEATER

Most of London's theaters were built on the south side of the Thames, away from the jurisdiction of the city authorities who were worried that they were a fire and disease risk. Their worry was not unfounded. The

Globe theater, built by Richard Burbage in 1599, burned down in 1613 when a cannon being used in a play exploded.

Some Londoners were more concerned with the moral and political danger of the theater rather than the physical risk of attending plays. Puritans accused the theaters of drawing people away from churches because Sunday was a popular time for plays. People were becoming more interested in watching a three-hour play and less willing to spend time in church listening to a one-hour sermon! Puritans also claimed that plays were a corrupting influence that encouraged immorality. They felt that women, especially, should avoid plays for fear of ruining their character.

Meanwhile, the city authorities feared that theaters gave people the opportunity to meet and plot against the government. They believed that plays encouraged idleness and closely packed the-aters led to the spread of disease. In order to gain

This 1560 panoramic map of London shows the river Thames flowing through the middle of the city. A series of bridges con-nects the City of London (north bank) to Southwark (south bank). A bridge has existed across the Thames in London for nearly 2,000 years. Then as now, the Thames served as a port for goods and visitors—including royalty—arriving in and leaving town. It was also the main highway within the town, providing a means of transportation across town that was often faster than the crowded, narrow, and muddy streets.

control over the potentially dangerous content of the plays themselves, the position of master of the revels was created to censor plays and advise Elizabeth and the Privy Council on their suitability for public audiences. The concern dealt less with immorality and violence than with censoring anything that might encourage political unrest. In 1597, Elizabeth and her ministers responded to Puritan and city council pressure by closing the theaters. Soon, however, there was a public outcry, and the theaters were reopened and even more were built.

MUSIC AND PAINTING

In Elizabethan England, musicians and painters also thrived. Many nobles and wealthy merchants wanted to entertain themselves and friends with music and have family portraits hanging in their houses.

Composers such as William Byrd and John Dowland wrote madrigals. These are four-part songs with lyrics usually concerned with the joys and sorrows of love. The music was often written along the four sides of a large piece of paper, so people could stand around a table to see and sing their separate parts. Church music also developed in the Elizabethan era. The medieval tradition of plainchant—unadorned melodies chanted by several people singing the exact same part—gave way to more polyphonic choral pieces, in which several vocal parts sang interweaving lines, producing beautiful and complex har- mony. Thomas Tallis was chief among this new generation of choral masters, and his works continue to be performed in churches and con- cert halls around the world.

Instrumental music was also pop- ular at home, and

This stringed instrument is known as an orpharion and was supposedly made for Elizabeth I in 1580. It is very similar to a lute. Lutes were considered the perfect instrument for solo playing and to accompany the human voice.

people learned to play the lute and recorder, a sort of flute. Also common was a keyboard instrument, similar to a harpsichord, with strings that were plucked. It was called a virginal, possibly in honor of Queen Elizabeth, who owned one and often played it.

Nicholas Hilliard became well known as a pain- ter who produced miniature portraits. He painted the queen at least six times. His painting style became fashionable and many people commissioned his work. Around 1570, he was appointed court miniaturist and goldsmith by Elizabeth.

THE POOR

Between the time of Henry VII and the end of Elizabeth's reign, the population in England and Wales doubled from 2 to 4 million. This resulted in increased demand for both jobs and food. At the same time, the opportunity to make large profits in the woolen cloth trade encouraged farmers to switch from crop to sheep farming, so less food was produced. Enclosure of common land with hedges increased during this period, particularly in the Midlands, so ordinary people no longer had a place to graze animals. Enclosure also meant less labor was needed on the farms, so unemployment increased. Then, in the 1580s and 1590s, the country suffered from a series of bad harvests and plagues. All these factors led to price increases that made many people's wages too low to live on.

The Catholic monasteries, which had previously helped to feed and clothe the poor, were closed during Henry VIII's reign. Since there was no unemployment pay, health insurance, or retirement plans at this time, many people without work simply had to take to the streets and beg. These people were called vagabonds.

Throughout her reign, Elizabeth and her government tried to tackle the twin problems of poverty and vagabondage by passing various laws. As early as 1563, she passed the Act for the Relief of the Poor, requiring all local authorities to appoint a special collector of alms (donations to the poor), although contribution was voluntary. Later laws required all males between the ages of twelve and sixty to find jobs and not leave them without permission. Maximum wages were set by justices of the peace for different types of work. Rogues, vagabonds, and beggars were whipped and burnt through the right ear with a hot iron. Repetition of vagabondage or begging activity was punished with death.

Towns were required to supply the poor with raw materials to keep them employed. Houses of correction were created to give beggars work. Finally, in 1598, the Great Poor Law required all towns to raise taxes from their citizens for the relief of the poor. Vagabonds were punished by whipping and banishment from the country if they repeated the offense.

ELIZABETH AND MARY QUEEN OF SCOTS

CHAPTER 6

Mary Stuart was born in 1542 and was the great-granddaughter of Henry VII of England, Elizabeth's grandfather. Henry's daughter Margaret (Mary's grandmother) had married James IV of Scotland. Mary was therefore related to Elizabeth, who was Mary's senior by nine years. As a Catholic with a claim to the English throne, Mary posed a threat to Elizabeth.

At the age of sixteen, Mary had been married to Francis, the French dauphin (or heir to the French throne). When Francis died in 1560, Mary returned to Scotland to claim her Scottish throne. However, her ambition was also to gain the English throne. In 1562, three years into Elizabeth's reign, Mary wrote to Elizabeth suggesting that she should be regarded as the rightful successor to the English throne upon Elizabeth's death.

MARY'S TIME ON THE SCOTTISH THRONE

When nineteen-year-old Mary returned to Scotland following the death of her husband, Francis, she found that the Protestant Reformation had taken hold there, led by John Knox. She decided to take a practical approach to the situation and tried to create a tolerant society for both Protestants and Catholics.

Even at this early stage, Elizabeth regarded Mary as a threat, particularly if she remarried a member of the French Catholic aristocracy. Elizabeth's solution was to try to arrange a marriage between Mary and her own favorite, Robert Dudley, the Earl of Leicester. Her plan failed because Dudley was not keen on the idea, as he still held out hopes of marrying Elizabeth himself. In turn, Mary was not keen to marry Dudley, as she had fallen in love with Lord Darnley, a Scotsman. Darnley was a grandson of Henry VIII's elder sister, so their marriage in 1565 strengthened Mary's claim to the English throne.

Darnley was one of the lustiest, best-looking lads in Scotland, but he was also a womanizing

Mary Stuart, the daughter of King James V of Scotland, was born on December 7, 1542. Six days later, Mary's father died and she became an infant queen, thereafter known as Mary Queen of Scots. At this time, Scotland was torn between pro-English Protestant and pro-French Catholic factions. In 1558, Mary Queen of Scots tipped the balance by marrying a French prince, who became King Francis II the following year. After the death of the English queen Mary Tudor ("Bloody Mary"), many English Catholics tried to put Mary Queen of Scots on the English throne. Throughout Elizabeth I's reign, several plots were hatched to install Mary in her place as queen of England. In 1587, Elizabeth had Mary beheaded for her role in one such plot.

drunkard who gave Mary little support and resented not being given the title of king. Mary, who was often lonely, increasingly turned to her Italian secretary, David Riccio, for company and support. However, in March 1566, Darnley and another noble burst into Mary's private rooms, and in her presence, dragged Riccio out and murdered him.

Mary's reaction was extraordinary. Fearing the resulting scandal might inspire an uprising from the Scottish nobles, she fled from her palace at Holyrood, in Edinburgh, persuading a now sober and repentant Darnley to go with her. When the fuss died down, the pair returned as if nothing had happened. Publicly, the pair seemed to have made up. Mary was certainly pleased when, soon after, she gave birth to a son, the future James VI of Scotland. Meanwhile she was secretly falling in love with the Earl of Bothwell.

In 1567, Darnley caught smallpox and was taken to his house at Kirk O'Field, near Edinburgh. Mary visited her husband almost every night, but on February 9, her visit was brief, since she had to return to Edinburgh to attend a wedding. At two o'clock in the morning, a huge explosion destroyed the house, and Darnley and a manservant were found dead in the garden. On closer examination,

Holyrood Palace, in Edinburgh, Scotland, was the home of Mary Queen of Scots for most of her life. Founded initially as a monastery, the original abbey's ruins *(above)* can still be seen. Mary married two of her husbands in this abbey. Today Holyrood Palace is the queen's official residence in Scotland and is the setting for state ceremonies and official entertaining.

they were found to have been strangled. Mary and her lover, the Earl of Bothwell, were both suspected of the murders.

Mary vowed that the murderers would be found and punished. When the Earl of Bothwell was accused of the crime, Mary ordered a trial. Bothwell was found not guilty, and three months later, he and Mary were married. This was her biggest mistake. In the wake of the Darnley scandal, the Scottish nobles lost faith in their monarch and rebelled. This led to Mary's imprisonment and forced abdication in favor of her son, James. The Earl of Bothwell fled Scotland and ended his days, insane, in a prison in Denmark. Meanwhile, Mary also escaped in 1568 and fled to England, where she was held captive for the rest of her life.

THE NORTHERN REBELLION AND THE BABINGTON PLOT

Despite the fact that Mary was her relative, Elizabeth refused to meet Mary while she was held captive in England under suspicion of murdering her husband. A court of inquiry was set up and letters found in a casket were produced, which claimed to prove Mary's guilt. These casket letters may have been forgeries, however, so Mary's part in Darnley's murder remained a mystery.

Meanwhile, Mary became the focus of Catholic plots against Elizabeth. Elizabeth's secretary of state, Sir William Cecil, became involved in a power struggle with the Duke of Norfolk and his family. Norfolk was Catholic and opposed Cecil and his Protestant government. The duke feared that England's expansion overseas would bring England into a ruinous conflict with Spain, so he was keen to settle the question of succession. He reasoned that a Catholic monarch in England would bring about peace with Spain. In 1569, the duke demanded that Elizabeth nominate Mary to succeed her. When Elizabeth refused, the duke plotted

Elizabeth I (second from right) is seen receiving two Dutch ambassadors (kneeling at her feet) in this Dutch painting from 1585. The ambassadors came to discuss England's possible help in overthrowing Spanish Catholic rule of the Netherlands. The queen's favorite, Robert Dudley, Earl of Leicester, (second man standing at left) was made commander of the English forces sent to help the Netherlands' Protestant rebels. He would return two years later when Mary Queen of Scots (who appears seated at far left) was executed.

to marry Mary, and the queen sent him to prison for a time in the Tower of London.

The arrest of the duke sparked off a rebellion of Catholics in the north of England during November 1569. Their aim was to put Mary on the

throne. Troops led by the Earls of Northumberland and Westmorland seized various northern towns including Darlington, Richmond, and Ripon, and burned the homes and crops of Protestants. At Durham, they stormed the cathedral, tore up bibles and prayer books, and celebrated the Catholic Mass.

Government agents took Mary south for safety and held her at Tutbury Castle in Staffordshire. The royal army, led by Lord Sussex, arrived in York, where it awaited more troops sent by Lord Warwick. Meanwhile, the rebel earls continued south toward York, hoping to be joined by troops from Lancashire. None arrived, and the rebels turned north where they besieged and captured Barnard Castle, south of Durham. At this point, the royal army caught up with the rebels and chased them north to Carlisle, where Mary's Catholic supporters were beaten in the only real fighting of the rebellion.

After the defeat of the rebels, the Earl of Westmorland sailed to the Netherlands where, for thirty years, he worked for Philip II, the king of Spain, helping Philip plan his invasion of England. The earl died an old man in 1601. The Earl of Northumberland escaped to Scotland, where he was looked after by the regent of Scotland. When Elizabeth offered a ransom of £2000 for the earl, the regent turned him in. Elizabeth then had Northumberland beheaded at York. Hundreds of rebels were rounded up. Some were pardoned, some deprived of their lands, and one man from each rebellious village was beheaded.

No action against Mary was taken at this stage. Nevertheless, because Elizabeth had no children, Mary continued to be the obvious successor to the throne and therefore remained the focus of Catholic hopes and plots. For example, in 1571, the Duke of Norfolk again became involved in a plot, this time to help the Spanish invade England. Once the plan was discovered, he was beheaded.

In 1586, the Babington plot proved Mary's ulti-mate downfall. A leading Catholic named Anthony Babington was suspected of plotting a rebellion against Elizabeth. The queen's spy-master, Francis Walsingham, uncovered the plot by making it possible for Babington to send letters to Mary, who was held captive in Chartley Hall, Derbyshire. The letters between Babington and Mary were smuggled in and out of the hall in beer barrels, but were intercepted by Walsingham. Elizabeth finally had the evidence she needed against Mary.

MARY'S EXECUTION

Mary was taken to Fotheringay Castle in Northamptonshire, where she was put on trial, found guilty, and sentenced to death. At this point, Elizabeth hesitated to carry out the sentence. Politically, she had no option, as Mary was clearly a security threat. However, Elizabeth was not happy about killing a close relative and a fellow monarch. Even once she did finally sign the warrant, she changed her mind and refused to send it to Fotheringay. Eventually, William Cecil sent the warrant ahead without Elizabeth's consent, and Mary Queen of Scots was beheaded on February 8, 1587.

EXPLORATION AND THE SPANISH ARMADA

Until the mid-1500s, there was little English interest in exploring and trading with the world beyond Europe, but voyages of discovery increased during Elizabeth's reign. Elizabethan sailors were also important when it came to protecting England from foreign invasion. Henry VIII had developed the navy to some extent, but it was largely privateer English sailors who played a crucial role in defeating the armada (fleet) sent by the king of Spain in 1588 to invade England.

CHAPTER 7

VOYAGES OF DISCOVERY

England's traditionally strong cloth trade with the Netherlands decreased dramatically during Elizabeth's reign.

This was largely due to declining relations with the Spanish, who owned the Netherlands and the surrounding area of sea. This situation forced the English to find new countries with which to trade. At the same time, increased patriotism encouraged the English to challenge the Spanish in the race to find new trade routes and discover new lands. Also, many people in England came to see colonization abroad as the answer to the problems caused by a rising population.

Although the number of voyages of discovery increased during the reign of Elizabeth, overall the voyages were not very successful in achieving their aims. Sailors, such as Sir Martin Frobisher, hoped to find a new route to China by either going northwest around North America or northeast around Russia. Unfortunately, no such passage exists. Similarly, other sailors, such as Sir Francis Drake, failed in their goal to find a new "southern continent" in the Pacific. Finally, the founding of colonies during Elizabeth's reign largely failed. Sir Walter Raleigh settled colonists in Virginia in 1585 and 1587, naming the area after the queen who, because she was unmarried, was affectionately known as the Virgin Queen. The people of the first colony swiftly returned to England, and those in the second colony disappeared, probably killed by Native Americans.

This is a drawing of an Elizabethan-era galleon. It is the type of ship used by privateers (a legal sort of pirate) and explorers, including Sir Francis Drake. It was also the type of ship used by the English navy during the sea battle that resulted in the defeat of the Spanish Armada.

More significant developments in English trade under Elizabeth included the setting up of several trading companies. Started in 1581, the Turkey Company established trade with the Ottoman Empire. The Barbary Company was started by the Earl of Leicester in 1585 to trade with Morocco. Most important, the East India Company was established in 1600 to generate trade with east and southeast Asia, as well as India. Eventually, the company came to govern India up to the mid-nineteenth century.

Elizabeth's foreign policy was dominated by European affairs, so she was not prepared to give financial backing to world exploration. Nevertheless, Elizabeth did recognize that trade and exploration were vital to English interests. She was particularly supportive of the explorer Francis Drake. When he became the first Englishman to circumnavigate the world, between 1577 and 1580, Elizabeth knighted him onboard his boat, the *Golden Hind*.

SPAIN DECIDES TO INVADE ENGLAND

At the start of Elizabeth's reign, England and Spain were at peace and allied against France. King Philip II of Spain had even proposed marriage to Elizabeth. But during her reign, relationships between the two countries declined to the point that Philip ordered his great fleet, known as the Spanish Armada, to invade England.

In the Treaty of Tordesillas of 1494, the pope took a map of the world and drew a line down the middle of the Atlantic from north to south. He was dividing the world between Spain and Portugal and asking these two countries to spread the Catholic faith worldwide through their colonizing and exploring activities. Any new lands they found in their travels would be theirs to claim. All other nations exploring the world, including England, would be regarded as intruders to be dealt with as enemies. Drake's first taste of this undeclared war

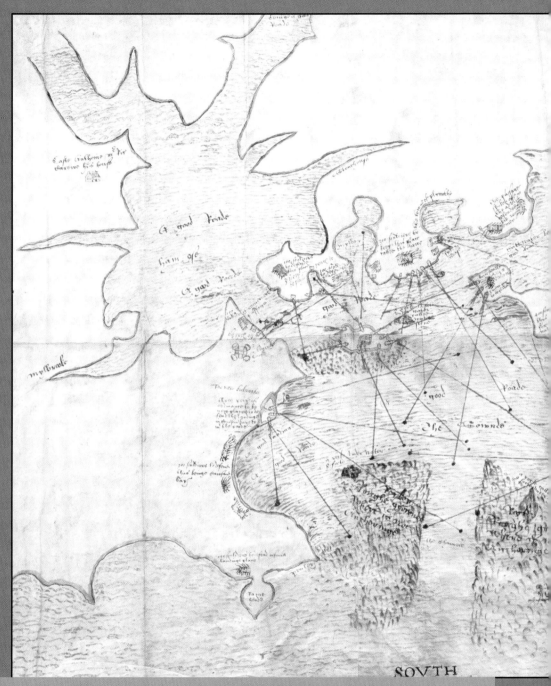

The above drawing is a sixteenth-century plan for the defense of Plymouth Sound, in Devon, England, against any potential attack from Spanish ships. Drawn on the map are soldiers firing muskets and cannons. The lines crisscrossing the plan indicate the range of these guns. The threat of an invasion of England by Spain was continuous throughout much of Elizabeth's reign, ending only with the defeat of the Spanish Armada in 1588.

was in 1568, off the coast of Mexico. Drake was accompanying his cousin John Hawkins on a slave-trading voyage when they were attacked by a Spanish fleet. Drake never forgot or forgave the Spanish for the unprovoked attack.

In the late 1560s, Spanish and English sailors engaged in an unofficial, undeclared war over trade and colonial expansion in the Americas. By the 1580s, Elizabeth was ordering English sailors, who became known as her sea dogs, to attack the Spanish treasure ships in the Caribbean. She was more than happy to receive the gold that sailors such as Drake brought back from the New World.

In addition to trying to put an end to this competition on the high seas, there were three other reasons why Spain decided to invade England. One reason involved Spain's rule of the Netherlands. In 1568, there was a Protestant revolt in the Netherlands against the Catholic Spanish rule, and Spain sent a large number of troops under the Duke of Alva to suppress it. Once these troops had suppressed the revolt, they posed a threat to England. Matters came to a head when five Spanish ships, carrying silver for the payment of Spanish troops in the Netherlands, took shelter from French privateers in the port of Southampton in the south of England. Elizabeth saw an opportunity and seized the silver, refusing to give it back. Then, in 1585, Elizabeth sent English troops commanded by the Earl of Leicester to help the Protestant rebels in the Netherlands. If Philip could successfully invade and subdue England, the danger of rebellion in the Netherlands would be greatly reduced.

A second reason Philip wanted to invade England was because recent military victories made the task much easier. In 1580, Philip annexed Portugal and seized its fleet. This victory provided the opportunity to transport troops to England for an invasion. However, in 1587, the year before the armada set sail, Drake set fire to old ships and let them drift into the Spanish harbor of Cadiz in order to destroy as much of the armada fleet as he could. Drake claimed he had "singed the king of Spain's beard" by destroying a reported thirty-seven ships.

A further reason Spain wanted to invade England involved the imprisonment of Mary Queen of Scots, and Philip's ambition to restore Catholicism to England. Philip preferred to have Elizabeth (even though he considered her a Protestant heretic) on the English throne, rather than Mary Queen of Scots, Elizabeth's obvious successor. This was because Scotland was allied with France. If Mary took the English throne, Spanish communications with the Netherlands would be threatened by an English-French military alliance. However, in 1568, Mary fled Scotland for England and was imprisoned by Elizabeth. This prompted the pope to excommunicate Elizabeth and urged Philip to invade England and restore the Catholic faith there. Elizabeth suspected that Philip was at the root of various plots against her life. In order to prevent any attempt by Philip to invade and install Mary as queen, Elizabeth signed Mary's execution order in 1587. The next year, Philip sent the armada to attempt an invasion of England.

THE DEFEAT OF THE SPANISH ARMADA

Philip's plan was to send 19,000 Spanish troops by boat to the Netherlands. There they would pick up 30,000 more troops commanded by the Duke of Parma (from the Spanish-controlled area of Italy)

The Spanish Armada was a fleet of ships sent out to invade England and put an end to the long series of English aggressions against Spanish colonies in the New World. However, this mighty fleet was defeated by a week's fighting with the British navy and disastrous sailing weather. When the armada set sail from Lisbon, Portugal, on May 20, 1588, it consisted of about 130 ships and 30,493 men. Half of these ships would be lost and three-quarters of the sailors would die during the ill-fated excursion. This marked the beginning of Spain's weakening as a maritime power.

and cross to England. Philip was certain that once Elizabeth was removed, he could put pressure on the English government to reconvert to Catholicism. The English did not have a regular army, so the Spanish felt they could invade without having to use much force. In reality, there were problems with the Spanish plan. Its chances of success were

slim, and Spain certainly underestimated the effectiveness of Elizabeth's sailors.

Spain's most experienced admiral died in January 1588, before the armada set sail. As a result, Philip appointed the Duke of Medina Sidonia to command the expedition, even though the duke had no practical naval experience. With regard to the fleet itself, the Spanish ships were big cargo carriers, whereas the English ships were much smaller, faster, and more maneuverable. The English cannons could be loaded and fired faster than the Spanish cannons. Some of the Spanish cannons had been cast just before the armada set sail and proved to be defective. They often exploded when fired. The Spanish traditionally fought by attaching themselves with grappling hooks to enemy boats and then boarding, but the English boats kept far enough away to prevent the Spanish from using this tactic. Most important, the English seamen knew the channel's currents and winds well. Finally, Philip ignored the fact that the Spanish did not have a suitable deep-water port in the Netherlands for the armada to enter and pick up Spanish troops.

On July 29, 1588, the armada was sighted in a close crescent formation off the coast of the Isles of Scilly. The English fleet left Plymouth to meet the enemy and got windward of the Spanish. The English then followed the armada up the channel, "plucking their feathers," or, in other words, picking off straggling ships. On August 2 and 3, inconclusive engagements were fought off the south coast of England near the Isle of Wight. The English divided into four squadrons, led by Lord Howard, Drake, Sir Martin Frobisher, and Hawkins, and prevented the Spanish from landing on the English coast. The armada continued to Calais where it waited for word from the Duke of Parma in the Netherlands. Eventually, the Duke of Medina Sidonia received word that the Spanish troops would not be able to join the armada for another two weeks. At this point, the English once again sent fire ships into the armada, breaking its formation. This allowed the English to engage and seriously damage the Spanish in the Battle of Gravelines on August 8.

The remaining armada ships were saved by a southerly wind and sailed north up the east coast of England, chased by the English, who returned home when they ran out of supplies. The armada originally

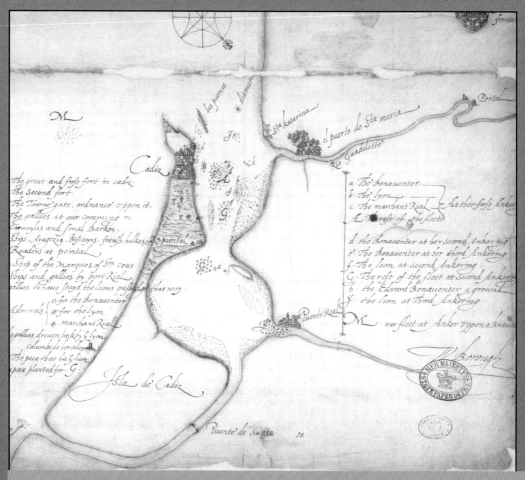

Philip II's first attempt to build an armada that would launch an invasion of England was thwarted in April 1587, when Sir Francis Drake entered the harbor of Cadiz where the Spanish fleet was stationed. In a surprise attack, Drake's twenty-three English vessels destroyed or captured thirty-eight of the Spanish ships that were to make up the armada. After Drake attacked and seized even more ships off the Portugal coast, Philip had to delay and revise his attack strategy. Above is a plan of Cadiz showing the positions of English and Spanish warships.

set sail with 130 ships. Only about seventy ships returned to Spain. Many of the missing Spanish ships were shipwrecked off the stormy coast of Scotland and Ireland on their long journey home.

Services of thanksgiving were held in England, and the words "God blew and they were dispersed" were printed on the commemorative medal given out to the victorious sailors. Elizabeth used the occasion of the defeat of the Spanish Armada to boost her status. On August 18, she visited the Earl of Leicester's army at Tilbury docks, where she made one of her most famous speeches. According to one of her chaplains, who wrote down what she said, Elizabeth declared, "I am come amongst you as you see, at this time, not for my own recreation and disport, but being resolved, in the midst and heat of battle, to live or die amongst you. I know I have the body of a weak and feeble woman, but I have the heart and stomach of a king, and of a king of England too, and think foul scorn of Parma, or Spain, or any prince of Europe should dare to invade the borders of my realm."

Though its mighty armada had been defeated, Spain continued to be a threat throughout the remainder of Elizabeth's reign. Elizabeth continued to send troops in support of the Protestants in the Netherlands, who had limited successes against their Spanish oppressors. She also sent English sea captains to destroy Spanish ships, burn ports, and seize Spanish treasure, but many of these expeditions were failures. Meanwhile, peace was sought with France in order to provide a counterbalance in Europe against the Spanish.

On the positive side, the confidence of English sailors had grown. England was starting to become a great seafaring nation, with a corresponding increase of trade, colonial expansion, exploration, and sea power.

In 1588, on the occasion of the defeat of the Spanish Armada, Nicholas Hilliard, court miniaturist and portraitist, created this locket bearing Elizabeth I's likeness. It is now housed in the Victoria and Albert Museum in London.

THE END OF THE ELIZABETHAN ERA

Although Elizabeth surrounded herself with loyal favorites who were devoted to serving her, one exception in Elizabeth's court was Robert Devereux, the Earl of Essex (1567–1601). His quest for power climaxed in 1601 with a failed rebellion. In dealing with the threat posed by the Earl of Essex, it is evident that the elderly queen showed signs of weakness and misjudgment.

CHAPTER 8

ESSEX AT THE QUEEN'S COURT

The background and personality of the Earl of Essex brought him to early prominence in Elizabeth's court. Most important, he was the stepson of the queen's earlier favorite, the Earl of Leicester. In addition, he had been brought up in the house-hold of William Cecil, and he was distantly related to the queen, being descended from her aunt Mary Boleyn. When he came to court in 1584 at the age of seventeen, the queen was taken with his looks, charm, and wit.

The queen and the Earl of Essex were soon spending a consider-able amount of time with each other and often played cards together late into the night. Elizabeth con-ferred various awards upon him, including making him a knight of the Garter (the highest and most sought after chivalric honor) at the age of twenty-one. How-ever, the Earl of Essex

Robert Devereux, Earl of Essex (*above*), became the queen's favorite late in her life. On her behalf, he led English forces against the queen's enemies in France, Spain, and Ireland. He eventually fell from favor and launched a failed rebellion against Elizabeth for which he was executed.

was hot-tempered and frequently argued with the queen. He became extremely jealous when the queen showed favoritism to anybody else.

Later, the earl tried to increase his power and popularity with the queen by undertaking a series of military expeditions. These took him to the Netherlands, France, and Spain. When he commanded land forces that captured Cadiz in 1596, the Earl of Essex became a national hero. The next year, however, he failed in an attempt to capture a Spanish treasure fleet.

In politics, Elizabeth had previously balanced the opposing followers of William Cecil and the Earl of Leicester against each other. Later, William Cecil was replaced as secretary of state by his son Robert. From this point on, the court and government became increasingly divided in their support for either Robert Cecil or the Earl of Essex, as the queen lost her grip on the earl's growing ambition.

ELIZABETH'S IRISH POLICY

Spain was not the only nation to present Elizabeth with difficulties. Ireland, with its heavily Catholic population, was a problem for Elizabeth for two reasons. First, its people had always resented English settlers in their land and English rule or "overlordship" since Henry II's conquest of Ireland in the twelfth century. Second, the English feared that the Spanish might help the Irish in their struggle against English rule and use Ireland as a base from which to mount an invasion of England.

In 1155, Pope Adrian IV had given King Henry II overlordship of the island, but in practice, the English always found it hard to control the Irish tribesmen. During the reign of Henry VIII the monasteries in Ireland were closed, but strong resistance to the idea of a Protestant reformation remained. During Elizabeth's reign, the English tried to solve all the problems in Ireland by adopting a policy of "grant and plant" in an attempt to colonize Ireland. The aim was to take land from the native Irish and "grant" it to Protestant English and Scottish settlers. However, as soon as the English troops left the new settlements, the Irish attacked the transplanted Protestant farmers.

Matters came to a head in 1598, when a powerful Irish chief, Hugh O'Neill, the Earl of Tyrone, rose in rebellion and destroyed an English army at the Battle of Yellow Ford. The Earl of Essex was keen to go to Ireland and crush the rebellion, hoping this would increase his prestige at court. When he heard that the queen was planning to send someone else, an argument followed. The Earl of Essex turned

Irish rebel Hugh O'Neill, Earl of Tyrone, formed an alliance with other Irish chieftains and the Spanish to fight against Elizabeth I. When he was defeated, he fled to Flanders.

his back on the queen (a severe breach of royal etiquette), who boxed him around the head, whereupon the Earl of Essex reached for his sword. Though he regained his composure and did not harm Elizabeth, the Earl of Essex was forbidden to be in the queen's presence again after this incident. Even so, the queen continued to favor him. He was sent to Ireland with 16,000 troops and 1,300 cavalrymen (the largest force ever to leave England during Elizabeth's reign) with instructions to defeat the Earl of Tyrone. His future at court depended on success in Ireland.

When the Earl of Essex arrived in Ireland, he spread his troops out to defend various towns against rebel attacks. Unfortunately, this left him with too few troops to attack the Earl of Tyrone, so his generals advised him to wait. Elizabeth sent a letter criticizing the Earl of Essex for this delay, at which point he signed a truce with the Earl of Tyrone and, against the queen's wishes, returned to England. His campaign had cost £300,000 and failed to achieve Elizabeth's goal of forcing the Irish to submit to her rule.

Back in England, the Earl of Essex hurried straight to the queen's bedchamber and entered before she was properly dressed. He was received but arrested afterward. Although he was shortly released from prison, it may be at this point that he started to plot his rebellion. Meanwhile, Lord Mountjoy was sent to Ireland, where, in 1601, he successfully defeated the Irish army and the Spanish troops sent to support rebellion.

THE DOWNFALL OF THE EARL OF ESSEX AND THE REBELLION OF 1601

The earl's personal finances were also a source of tension between him and the queen. The Earl of Essex's father, the Earl of Leicester, had spent most of the family fortune during his own unsuccessful military expedition to Ireland in 1573. The Earl of Essex therefore relied heavily on his monopoly on the importation of sweet wine, granted to him (and previously to his father) by the queen. The royal finances became increasingly strained as costly foreign

Elizabeth I is shown on horseback on this great seal engraved by Nicholas Hilliard in 1584. The inscription around the edge reads in Latin "Elizabeth, by grace of God, Queen of England, France and Ireland, Defender of the Faith."

wars and inflation took their toll. As a consequence, Elizabeth was less generous with the granting of royal patronage, or the giving of favors, land, or business opportunities. In 1600, following the earl's disastrous expedition to Ireland, the queen withdrew his wine monopoly and with it his financial security. This snub must have fuelled the Earl of Essex's plan to rebel.

The Earl of Essex had fallen from favor with the queen and faced charges of treason from Robert Cecil. He seemed doomed unless he could overthrow Cecil. With his remaining supporters, he therefore aimed to start a rebellion in London and then clear the city of his opponents.

On February 8, 1601, the Earl of Essex entered London with 300 supporters, including three earls and three barons. The members of the Privy Council who met him were taken hostage. The Earl of Essex falsely declared that the queen was in danger from a

Spanish plot and urged people to join his mission to save her. The city authorities did indeed raise troops, but instead of supporting the earl, they surrounded his men and arrested him.

Even if this plot did not aim at overthrowing the queen, it was obvious that Elizabeth could not tolerate this sort of behavior. She acted decisively. The Earl of Essex was tried for treason and executed on February 25, 1601, at the age of thirty-four.

Until her decision to have him executed, Elizabeth had long showed weakness and misjudgment in much of her dealings with the Earl of Essex. He had an inflated opinion of himself, was hotheaded, jealous of favoritism shown to others, argumentative, power-hungry, and difficult to control. Even so, the queen mourned his death and continued to wear the ring he had given her until the day she died.

THE QUESTION OF SUCCESSION

As it became increasingly clear that Elizabeth would not marry, she came under intense pressure to name her successor. During the reigns of both her father and half-sister, she had learned the problems that marriage could pose to a ruler. As an unmarried queen, however, she also learned

In this portrait, Elizabeth is uncharacteristically depicted in relatively plain clothes and a simple background. Unlike many of her portraits, there is little attempt to project a public image or create allegorical meanings. One of the few obvious emblems of her royalty is the ermine collar she wears. Ermine, a kind of mink, was a symbol of royalty, and its fur was often used to trim royal robes.

how dangerous it was to let support gather around an accepted or apparent heir to the throne who might be impatiently waiting in the wings. By deciding not to marry, it seems as if she had traded stability within her lifetime for instability at the end of her reign.

Elizabeth did all she could to stifle debate on the question of succession. In the end, of course, she outlived all rival claimants, or, as in the case of Mary Queen of Scots, she simply removed them. At the same time, her reluctance to name an heir encouraged people to be loyal to her by focusing their attention on the importance that her own reign should continue. She was also fearful that if an heir were named too early, attention and loyalty would be transferred from her to the future monarch as she grew older. She feared the possibility that the named successor might try to seize power before her death.

THE QUEEN IS DEAD

By the time she lay dying in 1603, Elizabeth was unable to speak and merely signaled her agreement that James VI of Scotland should succeed her as king of England. When she died in her sleep, at 3:00 AM on March 24, a messenger rode to James in Scotland, carrying a ring that the future king had once given

On March 24, 1603, at Richmond Palace, Elizabeth I died. This illustration depicts the funeral procession of Queen Elizabeth I, including her effigy placed on top of the coffin.

Elizabeth. The ring served as proof both that Elizabeth had died and that she supported James's ascension to the throne.

Elizabeth's body was taken by boat down the river Thames from her palace at Richmond for burial at Westminster Abbey, the final resting place of many of England's kings and queens. A realistic effigy of the queen was placed on the coffin as it was carried through the streets. The crowds that turned out to pay their last respects were visibly upset. The queen who had pacified and unified England and made it a dominant worldwide power during a long and successful reign was suddenly gone. The Elizabethan age was at an end.

TIMELINE

January 25, 1533	Henry VIII marries Anne Boleyn.
September 7, 1533	Elizabeth is born at Greenwich Palace to Anne Boleyn and Henry VIII.
May 19, 1536	Anne Boleyn, Elizabeth's mother, is beheaded when Elizabeth is just two-and-a-half years old.
January 1547	Henry VIII dies. His son Edward VI takes the throne at the age of nine.
July 6, 1553	Edward VI dies at the age of fifteen and is succeeded two weeks later by Mary Tudor.
March 18, 1554	Elizabeth is sent to the Tower of London under suspicion of plotting against Mary Tudor.
November 17, 1558	Mary Tudor dies and is succeeded by Elizabeth.
January 15, 1559	Elizabeth is crowned.
1559	Elizabeth develops her Protestant/Catholic religious settlement.
April 8, 1559	Parliament passes the Act of Supremacy, restoring Protestantism in England. Elizabeth becomes head of the Church of England.
1561	Mary Stuart takes the throne of Scotland following the death of her husband, French king Francis II. She becomes known as Mary Queen of Scots.
1568	Elizabeth imprisons Mary Queen of Scots.
1569	The Northern Rebellion attempts to put Mary Queen of Scots on the throne.

TIMELINE *[continued]*

1570 Pope Pius V excommunicates Elizabeth.

1572 Elizabeth names William Cecil as High Lord Treasurer.

1575 Robert Dudley, the Earl of Leicester, entertains Elizabeth at Kenilworth Castle.

1579 Elizabeth's marriage negotiations with the French king's brother, the Duke of Alençon, collapse.

1580 Pope Gregory XIII declares that anyone who kills Elizabeth would not be committing a sin.

April 4, 1581 Queen Elizabeth knights Sir Francis Drake after he sails around the world.

1586 The Babington Plot is foiled. The plotters hoped to replace Elizabeth with Mary Queen of Scots.

February 8, 1587 Mary Queen of Scots is executed.

April 1587 Francis Drake attacks the Spanish fleet at Cadiz.

July 1588 King Philip II launches the Spanish Armada in the hope of invading England.

August 8, 1588 English fleets defeat the Spanish Armada.

1588 Robert Dudley, the Earl of Leicester, dies.

1598 William Cecil dies.

February 25, 1601 Robert Devereux, the Earl of Essex, is executed after an apparent attempt at revolt.

March 24, 1603 Queen Elizabeth dies and is succeeded by James VI of Scotland.

GLOSSARY

abdication The stepping down from power of a king or queen.

casket A storage box, usually small and made of wood.

Catholic A Christian who accepts the leadership of the pope. In the Middle Ages, all European Christians were Catholic. After the Reformation, those who broke away from the Catholic Church and the pope's authority became known as Protestants.

circumnavigation The sailing of a ship around the world.

colonization The creation of a new territory by an established state. The colony is governed by the parent state.

forgeries False documents that are made to fool people into thinking they are legitimate.

heretic Somebody who rejects the teachings of an established church.

monarch A king or queen.

monastery A complex of buildings in which a community of monks live, work, worship, and pray.

Netherlands An area of Europe now occupied by Holland, Belgium, and Luxembourg.

nobles Earls and lords, often related to the monarch.

overlord A monarch or noble who rules an area.

Parliament The United Kingdom's legislative assembly of nobility, clergy, and commoners called together by the British king or queen.

persecution The victimization of a person or group of people for their beliefs.

privateer A privately owned ship that takes part in armed action against the commercial ships of enemy nations, usually on behalf of a government or ruler.

Protestant A member of any of several Christian denominations that deny the authority of the pope and support the Reformation principles first put forth by sixteenth-century religious leaders such as Martin Luther and John Calvin, who broke away from the Catholic Church.

smallpox A contagious disease that involves fever, skin eruptions, and scarring.

succession The transition from one ruler to another.

tuberculosis An infectious and potentially fatal disease of the lungs.

FOR MORE INFORMATION

The British Museum
Great Russell Street
London, England WC1B-3DG
(011) 44-20-7323-8299
Web site: http://www.thebritishmuseum.
  ac.uk

Palace of Holyrood House
Foot of Royal Mile
Edinburgh, Scotland EH8-8DX
(011) 44-131-556-7371
Web site: http://www.royal.gov.uk/output/
  page559.asp

The Tower of London
London, England EC3N-4AB
(011) 44-870-756-6060
Web site: http://www.hrp.org.uk/webcode/
  tower_home.asp

WEB SITES

Due to the changing nature of Internet
links, the Rosen Publishing Group, Inc.,
has developed an online list of Web sites
related to the subject of this book. This
site is updated regularly. Please use this
link to access the list:

http://www.rosenlinks.com/rsar/eliz

FOR FURTHER READING

Ashby, Ruth. *Elizabethan England.* Salt Lake City, UT: Benchmark Books, 1999.

Ashworth, Leon. *Queen Elizabeth I.* Slough, England: Evans Brothers Ltd., 2002.

Gardiner, Juliet. *Who's Who in British History.* London: Collins and Brown, 2000.

Guy, John. *Elizabeth I and the Armada.* Tonbridge, England: Ticktock Publishing Ltd., 2001.

Havelin, Kate. *Queen Elizabeth I.* Minneapolis: Lerner Publications Co., 2002.

Hilliam, David. *Kings, Queens, Bones and Bastards.* Stroud, England: Sutton Publishing, 1998.

Lace, William W. *Elizabeth I and Her Court.* San Diego, CA: Lucent Books, 2002.

Langley, Andrew. *Shakespeare and the Elizabethan Age.* Philadelphia: Running Press, 2000.

Langley, Andrew. *The Tudors.* London: Heinemann, 1994.

MacDonald, Fiona. *The Reformation.* Austin, TX: Raintree/Steck Vaughn, 2002.

Price-Groff, Claire. *Queen Elizabeth I.* San Diego, CA: Lucent Books, 2000.

Snellgrove, Laurence Ernest. *The Early Modern Age.* New York: Longman, 1997.

Stanley, Diane. *Good Queen Bess: The Story of Elizabeth I of England.* New York: HarperCollins, 2001.

Stewart, Gail B. *Life in Elizabethan London.* San Diego, CA: Lucent Books, 2002.

Styles, Sue. *Elizabethan England.* Oxford, England: Heinemann Educational, 1999.

Thomas, Jane Resh. *Behind the Mask: The Life of Queen Elizabeth I.* New York: Clarion Books, 1998.

Woog, Adam. *A History of Elizabethan Theater.* San Diego, CA: Lucent Books, 2002.

BIBLIOGRAPHY

Black, J. B. *The Reign of Elizabeth.*
Oxford, England: Clarendon
Press, 1952.

Brimacombe, Peter. *All the Queen's Men:
The World of Elizabeth I.* New York:
Palgrave Macmillan, 2000.

Dunn, Jane. *Elizabeth and Mary:
Cousins, Rivals, Queens.* New York:
Knopf, 2004.

Erickson, Carolly. *Bloody Mary.* New
York: St. Martin's Griffin, 1998.

Fraser, Antonia, ed. *The Life and Times
of Elizabeth I.* New York: Cross River
Press, 1992.

Fraser, Antonia. *Mary Queen of Scots.*
New York: Delta, 1993.

Guy, John. *Queen of Scots: The True Life
of Mary Stuart.* New York: Houghton
Mifflin Co., 2004.

Haigh, Christopher. *Profiles in Elizabeth
I.* New York: Longman, 1988.

Hibbert, Christopher. *The Virgin Queen:
Elizabeth I, Genius of the Golden Age.*
Boston: Addison-Wesley Publishing
Co., 1992.

Hilliam, David. *Crown, Orb and Sceptre.* Stroud, England: Sutton Publishing, 2001.

Jack, Sybil. *Towns in Tudor and Stuart Britain.* Basingstoke, England: Macmillan Press, 1996.

Reeves, Marjorie. *Elizabethan Court.* London: Longman, 1984.

Ridley, Jasper. *Bloody Mary's Martyrs: The Story of England's Terror.* New York: Carroll & Graf, 2002.

Rowse, A. L. *The Elizabethan Renaissance: The Cultural Achievement.* Chicago: Ivan R. Dee, Inc., 2000.

Rowse, A. L. *The England of Elizabeth.* Madison, WI: University of Wisconsin Press, 2003.

Strachey, J. *The Rolls of Parliament.* London: The Records Commissioners, 1767–1832.

Weir, Alison. *Elizabeth the Queen.* London: Random House UK, 1998.

Weir, Alison. *The Life of Elizabeth I.* New York: Ballantine Books, 1999.

Williams, Neville. *The Life and Times of Elizabeth I.* New York: Stewart, Tabori, & Chang, 2000.

INDEX

ABOUT THE AUTHOR

Paul Hilliam is a graduate of London University. He is Senior Master at Derby Grammar School in England, where he enjoys teaching history and religious studies. He has traveled throughout Europe, the Middle East, and India visiting sites of historical interest.

CREDITS